HUNTING with Flushing Dogs

By Joe Stetson

Distributed in the U.S.A. by T.F.H. Publications, Inc., 211 West Sylvania Avenue, P.O. Box 27, Neptune City, N.J. 07753; in England by T.F.H. (Gt. Britain) Ltd., 13 Nutley Lane, Reigate, Surrey; in Canada by Clarke, Irwin & Company, Clarwin House, 791 St. Clair Avenue West, Toronto 10, Ontario; in Southeast Asia by Y. W. Ong, 9 Lorong 36 Geylang, Singapore 14; in Australia and the south Pacific by Pet Imports Pty. Ltd., P.O. Box 149, Brookvale 2100, N.S.W., Australia.
Published by T.F.H. Publications, Inc. Ltd., The British Crown Colony of Hong Kong.

Cover photo by Joe Stetson

Frontispiece: The sport of hunting with flushing spaniels brings pleasure and wholesome recreation to many. Hartwell S. Moore, famous supporter of the American Cocker in the field, poses after a successful hunt with Field Ch. Berol's Buckaroo. Photo by Evelyn Shafer.

ISBN 0-87666-293-9

©1965 by **TFH** PUBLICATIONS, INC.   P.O.Box 27,   Neptune City, N.J. 07753

Contents

1. PURPOSE AND DESCRIPTION 5
   What is a Flushing Dog? . . . What Breeds are Eligible? . . . How Should a Flushing Dog Work? . . . Hunting Versus Field Trials

2. TERMINOLOGY 12

3. OBTAINING THE DOG 15
   Choosing a Breed . . . Introduction to the Family

4. THE CAR AND THE DOG 19
   Combating Carsickness . . . Teaching Travel Manners . . . Travel Precautions

5. PRELIMINARY TRAINING 22
   Yard Training . . . Collar and Lead . . . Sit or Hup . . . Recall

6. RETRIEVING 27
   Force Training to Retrieve . . . Steadiness Before Retrieve . . . Water Work

7. SOME COMMON FAULTS AND HOW TO CORRECT THEM .. 36
   Hard Mouth . . . Curing Hard Mouth . . . Freezing . . . Remedy For Freezing

8. DIRECTION SIGNALS 41

9. INTRODUCTION TO BIRDS 46
   Developing Hunting Enthusiasm . . . Game to Use for Experience . . . Planting Birds for Flushing . . . Practice Trailing Cripples

10. FINAL ESSENTIALS 56
    Hunting Pattern . . . Introduction to the Gun . . . Sport of Hunting With a Flushing Dog

The author with a young Welsh Springer Spaniel who has just retrieved his first pheasant.

1. Purpose and Description

WHAT IS A FLUSHING DOG?

A flushing dog is one which seeks game within range of the hunter's gun and, upon locating it, flushes it boldly into the open so the hunter may get a fair shot. Though the game may be cottontail rabbit or hare, it is more usually birds. The dog's duties are completed when the fallen game has been retrieved to the hunter's hand.

WHAT BREEDS ARE ELIGIBLE?

All spaniels, except the Brittany Spaniel, which is a pointing breed, are considered flushing dogs, but any dog trained to work like a flushing spaniel may be used as a flushing dog and is just as good as the job turned in, regardless of breed — mixed or otherwise. We often find members of the retriever family trained as flushing dogs and many an odd breed, such as the Collie, responds to the opportunity to flush game.

The spaniel breeds have been designed to range close to the gun, flush birds boldly, and retrieve the shot game to the hunter's hand.

In again, out again. Bold entries and prompt, soft-mouthed deliveries, such as these, indicate championship form. These English Springers, and those on the facing page, were captured in action at the National trials.

The heavier, slower Clumber Spaniel makes an excellent, close-working gun dog for the hunter who has slowed up, or likes to hunt in a more leisurely fashion. Photo by Louise Van der Meid.

Boldness, soft mouth, accurate eyesight and memory are a few of the things a dog must have to be useful in the hunting field.

The spaniels, however, are specialists, having been bred for centuries to do this job. Even before firearms, they were used to flush game for the falcon. The most commonly used spaniels are the English Springer, the English Cocker, the American Cocker, and the rather rare Welsh Springer, Field Spaniel, Sussex Spaniel, and Clumber Spaniel.

HOW SHOULD A FLUSHING DOG WORK?
It is essential that flushing dogs force game into the open or off the ground within gunshot. They must, therefore, work within range of the gun. Their ground pattern should be quite regular so as to leave no cover unhunted, but the pattern may be adjusted to variations in the cover and with consideration for direction and intensity of the wind.

To be valuable in such work the dog must have reasonable speed and endurance, a good nose, boldness to flush, a good sense of orientation, and willingness to hunt to the gun. Since retrieving the game is an essential part of a flushing dog's work, the eyesight and memory to watch a flight and mark a fall are necessary characteristics, as are willingness to negotiate any cover or body of water, good pickup, soft mouth, and good delivery to the hunter's hand. With respect to retrieving and ability to take instructions to hunt specially indicated pieces of cover, mastery of direction signals is important.

Willingness to retrieve is another vital quality a good flushing spaniel must have. This American Cocker clearly shows this positive attribute.

The spaniel has been described as "the ideal gentleman's shooting dog." He is capable of bringing outdoor enjoyment to his owner whether the interest is competition in trials or just fun.

Mrs. Henry Berol, one of the foremost breeders of field type American Cockers, accepts a retrieve from Field Ch. Berol Lodge Gay Lady. Despite his small size the American Cocker is still capable of bringing in heavy birds.

HUNTING VERSUS FIELD TRIALS

Considerable controversy usually results from comparing performance required in field trials with that desired of a dog in a day's hunt. There is a lot to be said about the differences when the subject is pointing dogs, retrievers or scent hounds. Flushing dogs, however, are another story. With the exception of the possibility that field trial judges may look with approval at just a bit more spark and something closer to the fringe of control, a top field trial dog and a top shooting dog are one and the same.

A field trial spaniel should be an ideal gentleman's shooting dog for locating and flushing birds to the gun, marking their fall and retrieving to hand upon command. Qualities should include desire, speed, stamina, nose, marking ability, and orientation steadiness, retrieving over land or water, ability to take directions and willingness to work for the gun. These are the same qualities desirable for getting the job done with class in the hunting field.

It remains only to recognize the fact that some hunters, due to age, well being or inclination, are more agile than others and the speed of a man's dog, to make hunting a pleasure, should conform to his own.

We must also recognize the fact that the dog we have to work with may not have all the desired qualities, yet may be loyal and willing to do the best he can with what he's got. We must then adapt our training methods and requirements to suit.

2. Terminology

The following listing of hunting terms and their definitions is presented so that there will be no confusion regarding the exact meaning of terms used throughout succeeding portions of this book. The novice will thus find satisfaction rather than confusion as the terms are later encountered.

BACKCAST: A cast in the direction opposite the progress of the hunt.

BLINKING: Avoiding contact with game after locating its presence — probably to avoid any punishment the dog has come to associate with birdwork. It can be caused by overtraining or, more remotely possible, gunshyness.

BODY SCENT: The scent direct from the body of the game.

BREAK: The following of the flight of a bird after flush and, possibly, completing a retrieve before commanded to do so; also, the following of a runner or cripple out of range despite the commands of the handler. A properly trained flushing dog should "hup" (come to a stop and sit) upon flushing game or upon gunshot or in the event game is flushed by a bracemate.

CAST: The swing a dog makes as part of his pattern in seeking game.

CAST OFF: The releasing of the dog as he is sent on to make his first cast.

CONTROLLED BREAK: Breaking for a limited distance before coming to a stop voluntarily or upon command — a break that does not go all the way. Discussions on what constitutes a break or a controlled break would fill volumes. Interpretation should be made in full consideration of the terrain and the accompanying circumstances. If, for example, a dog moves to a place from which he can watch the flight and mark the fall of a bird that has placed a tree or other obstacle between itself and the dog by the direction of its flight — and stops of his own initiative — he should be considered as having marked intelligently and not broken.

FALL: The actual fall of the shot game and the place where it came to earth whether killed or crippled.

FLASH POINT: An instantaneous point after which the dog flushes of his own accord. Since any hesitation to flush is a fault in a flushing dog, this can be criticized, but the fault is a matter of degree. A second's pause upon recognition of the presence of game, especially if that moment is used to pinpoint the location for a bold flush, can certainly not seriously affect a dog's work.

FREEZING: Failing to give up a retrieve freely.

GROUND SCENT: The scent left by game on the ground or on grasses or other growth against which it brushes.

The field dog enthusiast has his own language. Once the novice hunter is acquainted with this, he will understand all of the confusing terms and phrases. Photo by Evelyn Shafer.

GUNSHY: Afraid of gunfire.

HACKING: Overhandling — giving too many commands — usually to the detriment of the dog's work, certainly to the detriment of his development and initiative.

HARD MOUTH: Clamping down too tightly on retrieves — sometimes even chomping on them. A dog who has trouble with a difficult cripple and somehow damages the bird while bringing it in should not be convicted of hard mouth on this basis alone.

MAKING GAME: The accelerated action of a dog, noticed especially in the activity of his tail as he becomes aware of the presence of game and goes about locating and flushing it.

PUNCHING: Repeatedly working out to and beyond the limits of the gun despite the efforts of the handler to keep the dog working effectively within convenient range.

STEADY TO WING AND SHOT: Remaining in the hup, or sit, position following a flush and shot or, if the flush was not witnessed by the dog, the shot alone. An unobserved flush might be that of a bracemate or one of the hunting party, or the dog might even cause a bird to flush but be turning away from it at the time, or the flush might be far out and screened by cover.

NYLABONE® is a necessity that is available at your local petshop (not in supermarkets). The puppy or grown dog chews the hambone flavored nylon into a frilly dog toothbrush, massaging his gums and cleaning his teeth as he plays. Veterinarians highly recommend this product . . . but beware of cheap imitations which might splinter or break.

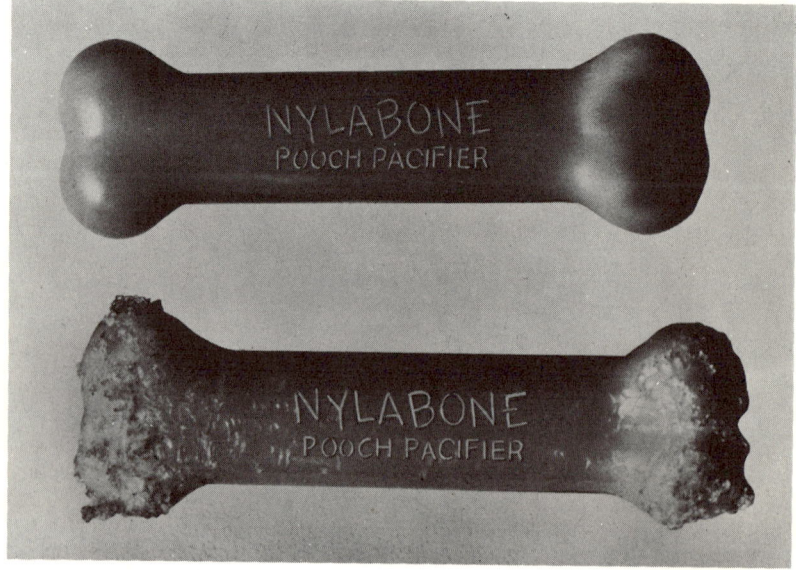

3. Obtaining The Dog

CHOOSING A BREED

It may be that, regardless of the breed, you already have the dog you wish to train to flush game for you in the field. If not, you may know just which breed you favor. Should you be in doubt about this, it would be a good idea to see a few dogs work in the field. Friends and neighbors may have breeds you would enjoy hunting over. If you are still in doubt, attend a field trial and watch the dogs work. English and American Cockers run together in Cocker trials. Springer trials are more numerous, but Cocker stakes are often run in conjunction with them. Remember! Regardless of the type of dog you use to flush birds for the gun, the method of running them and the means for training them have been perfected over many years. These methods or something close to them are well worth using as a model.

When you have decided which breed you wish to acquire, contact breeders of the dogs you have seen work and liked. It may be that your budget is limited and you cannot afford a pup from breeders of winning dogs, but start your inquiries there and move on to references given you by successful breeders.

These English Springer puppies are the result of a careful blending of hunting strains. Proper management and training will help make them top performers in the hunting field when they grow up.

Field Ch. Fast, owned by Mrs. W. A. Morin. The English Springer has always been one of the favorite sporting dogs of American hunters. Photo by Percy T. Jones.

    Whatever dog you acquire should be of fearless temperament. Oversensitive dogs often have superior intelligence and sometimes develop into excellent gunning companions. If you already have a very sensitive — even a shy dog — you may very well be able to bring him around successfully. There isn't much logic, however, in going out and getting trouble when you don't have it.

    Keep in mind that championship stock can be conformation as well as field winners. In looking for a hunting dog, be sure that you get a pup from field ancestry. The parents don't have to be champions, just good, honest working dogs. It is possible for conformation stock to be good in the field, but this is likely to be the exception rather than the rule. Most sporting dogs bred for the show ring, are less adept in the field. Make sure that such exceptions can be convincing at work.

The best field performers usually stem from dogs especially bred for hunting. The ability of these dogs in the field is second to none. Photo by Evelyn Shafer.

Style, skill, and a birdy carriage are the hallmarks of a top winning field trial spaniel such as Field Ch. Stoneybroke Sheer Bliss, owned by Philip D. Armour, Jr. and handled by Clifford Wallace. Photo by Evelyn Shafer.

Ten winsome Springer puppies pose with their parents. Each of them has the potentiality to become the invaluable hunting companion of an outdoorsman. Field & Stream.

A great deal has been said about how much or little a dog should cost. All these considerations, of course, must take into account each buyer's budget. Generally speaking, however, healthy stock that has been properly immunized is worth more. Then, too, the more training a dog has, the more it is worth. Keep in mind that a cheap dog eats as much as a more costly one. A higher first cost may be a lower long term purchase, especially where healthy, well-raised, and properly immunized puppies are concerned.

INTRODUCTION TO THE FAMILY

The start a dog gets in its new home is of vital importance. Though some bold, boisterous puppies may take over their new situation with no inhibitions whatsoever, others may be of a sensitivity or an age, or perhaps at a loss from leaving familiar surroundings, as to feel insecure during the all-important period of introduction.

It is good practice to ask the cooperation of all members of the family when the new member arrives. Excited, high-pitched voices and quick, pouncing movements such as are likely to greet a cute puppy should be avoided. Let the new arrival make the advances. Sit quietly and let him investigate his strange surroundings, and he will soon come to one and then another member of his new family and acquire a sense of security that will add greatly to his whole life with you.

4. The Car and The Dog

COMBATING CARSICKNESS

Some dogs adjust themselves to a car's sounds, motions, odors, or whatever makes other dogs nervous and carsick. If your dog is one of the unfortunates, he can best be cured by taking him on numerous short trips. To save trouble it is best to feed after the ride. The dog is thus rewarded at the end of the ride besides traveling on an empty stomach with less difficulty in case of accident. Be prepared for the worst: carry cleaning materials with you, but there is not likely to be trouble if the rides are short and gradually lengthened.

A good flushing spaniel should be serviceable for every kind of upland game bird, and for waterfowl as well. Photo by Evelyn Shafer.

It is a great help if a dog maintains good behavior in a car and can be taken from place to place by his owner, without difficulty. Photo by Louise Van der Meid.

Some hunters prefer to transport their dogs to and from the field by means of a pick-up truck. Care should be taken so that there is no chance for the dogs to escape. Photo by Louise Van der Meid.

TEACHING TRAVEL MANNERS

Allowing your dog to ride with his head out of the window is unwise because, at today's high speeds, it can result in eye inflammation and, moreover, it is sometimes the beginning of an inching process with the dog leaning further and further out the window until a curve or bump may cause him to fall out. I've seen it happen.

Car doors can be dangerous when closed without ascertaining that a foot, ear, or tail is not in a position to be injured.

Undisciplined dogs (and a car in motion is not the place to start discipline) can startle a driver or bump against him or even get jammed up in the wheel or pedals. Don't join those who have already come to grief because of a dog's unpredictable behavior while traveling in a car. At high speeds a slight swerve can mean a head-on collision.

TRAVEL PRECAUTIONS

Never leave a car in the sun with the windows closed. *Never* carry a dog in the trunk unless the trunk is equipped with an approved method of ventilation from an up-front location. Blocking the trunk lid open is worse than leaving it closed as exhaust gases containing carbon monoxide will be drawn in even quicker. The rear windows of station wagons should not be opened for ventilation unless the car is equipped with wind vanes on the outer corners to help satisfy the partial vacuum produced in the rear of a car in motion.

The ideal place for a dog in a car is in a crate designed for him and the car. Thus he will not damage upholstery or clothing no matter how muddy or wet. He will be safe with windows open. He can be kept warm in cold weather after a hunt in any combination of ventilation by the human passengers. Car windows can be kept open in hot weather while the dog is securely retained in his crate.

Never leave a gun where a dog may trigger it, in a car or anywhere else.

Dogs should be trained to wait for a command to enter or to leave a car. The former will save occupants from a muddy or a shedding scrambler, and the latter may save the dog's life by keeping him from bolting into traffic or other dangerous situations the moment the car door is opened. The car, as elsewhere, is a place where a disciplined dog can be a great satisfaction.

5. Preliminary Training

YARD TRAINING

The more routine training done without association with game the better. This is an opinion I base upon the fact that contact with game should be pleasant for the dog in order that his desire to hunt be dampened as little as possible by the inhibitions of training and such reprimand as may be necessary.

If, therefore, the dog is taught to sit (hup), walk at heel, come, retrieve, and take direction signals before being taken into the field, it will not only be much easier to handle him in the presence of game, but the edge of his enthusiasm will not be dulled.

COLLAR AND LEAD

If your dog is a puppy, you may have to accustom him to a collar and lead. It is best that he wear the collar for a while before you make use of it. After two or three days, snap the lead to the collar for a few minutes at a

Heeling on lead, as demonstrated by this English Cocker, should be a part of every dog's education prior to his field training. Photo by Louise Van der Meid.

Many useful hunting accessories, including special collars and leads, whistles, training scents, etc., are available to make each hunter's job easier in training his dog.

time and let him drag it around. Never leave a youngster alone with a collar for any length of time or he may get hung up, with the possibility of death by strangulation.

When the puppy is accustomed to collar and lead, pick up the end of the lead, and walk about with him for a bit, then, remembering that his span of attention is short, walk in straight lines with the idea of his walking with you. He will stray, walk slower and run faster, or even resent the lead and stop. You must teach him that it is pleasanter for him to walk with you than otherwise. Bring him to your side when necessary, but use short jerks, easing the lead when he is right and jerking in the necessary direction when he is not. He will soon learn that he is not jerked when he is walking at your side.

Each time you jerk the lead to bring him to you, repeat the command "heel." Talk pleasantly to him when he is going well. In very few short sessions he will be heeling nicely at your side.

Now, command "heel" and increase your speed, slow down, take right and left turns. It is not necessary to exaggerate these changes of direction and pace, but he should stay with you under reasonable circumstances. Praise helps a great deal.

When the dog performs perfectly on lead, unsnap the lead and work him similarly off lead. If need be, resort to the lead again. At first it is good practice to precede off-lead training with a short period of on lead practice.

Training the young dog should be done carefully so that the dog understands each successive step. In the early stages it helps to keep him on a light lead or check cord. Photo by Louise Van der Meid.

A check cord is helpful in training a young dog on the recall and retrieving. After he understands what is required of him, the cord can be discarded. Photo by Louise Van der Meid.

SIT OR HUP

The term used in the field to stop a dog, whether at heel or when a bird has been flushed or a gun fired is "hup." It is a good idea to use this term from the start if the dog is to be worked in the field.

RECALL

When your puppy is a short way from you and his attention is not on something else in particular, call his name and, as he looks at you, bow and step back a step or two as you lower your hands as though to receive a retrieve. Many puppies will come when you call, and go through these motions. If your puppy does, ask him to hup and then pat him, rub his ears or whatever seems to indicate best to the dog that he has pleased you. Repeat this at different distances and under different circumstances until the performance is perfect. It is now time to substitute a recall whistle for the command (name and "come"). Retriever trainers have used a long and two short trills satisfactorily for years. There is no reason why it won't do well with flushing breeds. I use it to recall all types of dogs. Repeat the command and whistle until the whistle alone will bring the dog in. Gradually you can stop stepping back, and of course when the dog is at a distance and not retrieving, the receiving-a-retrieve attitude need no longer be assumed.

Should the dog not respond naturally to your recall and gestures, you may resort to a check cord. Snap a twenty-foot length of light line, such as

When trouble is taken to train a young dog properly, the result will be a reliable hunting companion who will give unlimited hours of enjoyment in the hunting field.

clothes line, to the dog's collar. Command the dog to hup, then walk to the other end of the line. Now call the dog and pull the line in hand over hand until he can be hupped in front of you. Praise and pet him, then walk away, insisting that he stay hupped, and repeat. Do this until the dog comes without pulling the cord. Work frequently, but for short periods at a time. Even after the dog is responding, put the check cord on for the first attempt at each new training session until his performance is completely dependable.

6. Retrieving

Many dogs are natural retrievers. By tossing objects to retrieve, starting with short distances and retaining the dog's enthusiasm, you may be able to develop a reliable retriever without much training.

Several things should be kept in mind while teaching retrieving. Never command a dog to fetch when there is no object to retrieve. Until a dog is well taught, it is better not to send him to a difficult experience of this sort where there is considerable doubt on the dog's part as to what is expected of him. Don't use hard objects in training. If an object is hard it must be clamped on hard by the dog in order that he carry it. Soft objects can be held easily because the teeth get a hold in the easily made depressions they create. It is deplorable to see children, even adults, throwing stones for a dog to retrieve or catch with no concern for broken teeth. Make certain that every retrieve started is completed until a dog is fully trained. Don't play with a retrieve when the dog brings it for delivery. He must accept praise as the

Flushing spaniels are capable of efficient retrieves on land as well as water, and under any conditions of weather. Photo by Evelyn Shafer.

Field Ch. Cinar Spot of Earlsmoor, a top field English Cocker, delivers a bird to his owner, the well-known dog authority, Dr. S. B. Milbank.

This picture shows a well-educated retriever. Bad habits in the delivery of birds can be avoided if a dog is shown the right thing to do from the start.

reward for a clean and unhesitating delivery. In fact, don't ever play a tug of war with the dog under any circumstances. He may wish to start the game at a most inopportune time.

If a dog hesitates to return all the way with a delivery, take a step or two backward as he approaches. This, of course, is not acceptable performance in a field trial, though it is better than a hesitant delivery. It will, however, encourage a novice dog to return to the point where the delivery can be made and praise received. Should the dog be extremely slow or hesitant, turn and walk away as he approaches. The dog's usual reaction to this will be to get to you to retain the man-dog contact which is all-important to most dogs.

FORCE TRAINING TO RETRIEVE

Dogs that do not retrieve satisfactorily naturally, either because they just do not wish to retrieve or because they are undependable, must be force trained. Whereas the pressure method — on foot or ear — may be necessary, it is usually possible to force train with patience alone.

The retrieving buck, which is a piece of rolled-up cloth or burlap or, as commonly used by amateur and professional trainers today, a small-boat bumper, is placed in the dog's mouth while in sitting position, and he is encouraged to hold it by tapping him lightly under the chin if he lowers his head or lower jaw to drop it.

If training is properly conducted, the transition from retrieving buck to birds will be a smooth one.

When the dog will hold the buck indefinitely, for which he should be praised, hold it just under his mouth and say "fetch," or whatever command you decide to use. (Experienced trainers in trials often used the dog's name, spoken briskly.) The dog may reach for it. If he does, praise him, if not, lower his head to it and place it in his mouth, then hold his head up and praise him as he holds it. Do this until the dog will pick up the buck from the ground. You may then try it a foot and then two feet away, but stop if he is not completely willing, as it is best under such circumstances to continue the force method.

Now put a check line on the dog. Throw the buck a short distance. Take the dog to it while repeating the command. Follow through on the pick-up and return to the place of origin. Sit the dog and accept the delivery. It may be necessary to tap the dog under the chin while traveling to keep a "hold." This must be repeated until the dog performs without hesitation. Praise is necessary. If it fails, the pressure system may have to be resorted to.

A buck, as said before, can be of rolled cloth or burlap. Later, a small-boat bumper (make sure it is not old, watersoaked or paint soaked). To these, pheasant wings can later be tied to make the transition to birds. Scents are available to further simulate birds and help to make the transition and to help the dog to locate difficult retrieves. Need I say that the scent used (pheasant, quail, and duck are available) should be the same as the wings used to make the buck?

A good hunting spaniel should be dependable for all retrieves. A quail or pheasant can be shot over a pond, so water retrieves can become necessary, even with upland birds.

Praise is a vital element in training a dog to retrieve. His master's approval will stir his will to do better every time.

A well trained hunting spaniel represents great effort on the part of his breeder and his trainer. The true gun dog devotee considers such an animal invaluable. Photo by Evelyn Shafer.

When a puppy shows interest in bringing in birds, it is a sure sign that he will mature into a fine hunter. Photo by Louise Van der Meid.

There are few things in the world of sport that are as inspiring as the complete partnership of dog and man in a hunting field. Good training makes this so.

STEADINESS BEFORE RETRIEVE

A polished performer must not make a retrieve until commanded to do so. Care must be taken to make sure that a dog is retrieving enthusiastically before steps are taken to steady the dog. A great deal of harm can be done if the enthusiasm is lost in steadying.

To steady, hold the dog when throwing the buck while commanding "hup" (this may be accompanied by a single short whistle blast, which is used more conveniently at a distance.) Command the dog to fetch and repeat until the command and/or the single whistle will hold the dog in a sitting position until the command to retrieve is given.

Many trainers do not endeavor to steady a dog on retrieve until he is at least ten months of age. They do not wish to lessen the dog's desire to retrieve by any inhibitions whatsoever. A puppy might become confused. Many dogs have been ruined by endeavoring to steady too early.

This Springer is awaiting the command of his handler before making a retrieve. With a finished dog, such as this one, a bold, prompt retrieve is sure to follow the command.

The true test of a dog's willingness to retrieve is his skill in retrieving shot birds from rough water. Needless to say, difficult retrieves, such as these, should be avoided with young dogs.

WATER WORK

Retrieving over water sometimes comes very easily. Short retrieves from gradually sloping banks are best to start. If the dog takes to the water readily, longer retrieves and more difficult take-offs can be practiced. Care must be taken not to overdo this. Judgment as to circumstances such as fast water, tides, heavy seas, ice, and the like are advisable for the dog's safety, especially an inexperienced or unconditioned dog.

Many trainers condition their dogs by taking them for swims. A stable skiff is ideal for this and dogs often enjoy swimming along behind. Distances can be gradually increased. Again, good judgment should be used in determining how much is good for the dog.

7. Some Common Faults and How To Correct Them

It is only logical that game delivered to hand be delivered in condition for the table. Too tight a bite or intense chomping is, therefore, a fault to be avoided or, if it is encountered, cured.

CURING HARD MOUTH

The traditional cure for hard mouth is affected by cutting a few pieces of semi-stiff wire in lengths just short of the diameter of the buck or bird being used. Thrust them through in various directions so the dog can carry the buck comfortably if he does not bite down. Biting down brings about the discomfort caused by the ends of the wire and is usually enough to develop tender-mouth habits.

Field Ch. Prince Tom III, U.D., owned by Tom Clute. This American Cocker is one of the foremost field dogs of his breed. Tom shows his extremely soft-mouthed technique in retrieving a duck. Photo by Evelyn Shafer for Field & Stream.

To insure a soft mouth, it is advisable to work gradually up from smaller to larger birds. An inexperienced dog should not be made to pick up heavy birds or strong cripples. Photo by Louise Van der Meid.

Many dogs have the most delicate of mouths. Carrying eggs without breaking them is quite possible. I remember an experience that was a bit embarrassing, but so definitely indicative of the soft mouth of the dog. I was working the National Cocker Spaniel Champion, Prince Tom, on a television program. There was never a more willing or efficient worker despite his small size. I used a big cock pheasant for the retrieve and was surprised to find that Prince was dropping the bird repeatedly and looking like a sloppy novice. Later, when I examined the bird, which had been dead for several hours, I found that the slippery feathers on the hardened body of the heavy dead bird made it almost impossible for a hold by a tender-mouth dog with a mouth as small as Prince's. Had the bird been freshly killed and the flesh soft, his canine teeth would have made the indentations necessary for a hold. A mouth hard enough to carry the long-dead bird would have damaged the flesh of the fresh game.

In order to reduce the probability of a young dog acquiring a hard mouth from necessity it is better not to use heavy birds or dead birds that have become stiff and hard. Nor is it a good idea to present young dogs with the problem of overcoming the struggles of a strong cripple. Against such difficulties the young dog must exert more pressure and lose the valuable tenderness which is natural with most dogs at the start.

Retrieving should always have a pleasant association for the dog. In this way the likelihood of his developing retrieving faults is greatly reduced. Photo by George Pickow from Three Lions, Inc.

Freezing on retrieves comes from a reluctance, on the dog's part, to end the contact between himself and the hunter. There are a number of remedies for this, but the tendency should never be allowed to continue in a flushing spaniel.

FREEZING

Freezing is the term applied to the reluctance of a dog to deliver a retrieve to hand after having located and returned it. A dog need not be hard-mouthed to freeze. The two faults are different and, in my opinion, have different causes — and different remedies are required.

REMEDY FOR FREEZING

It is my thought that a dog freezes because he wishes to maintain contact with his handler. If and when he delivers the bird the contact is lost. With this in mind, I recommend endeavoring to minimize the importance of the delivery by distracting his mind from it. One way to do this is to toss out another buck just as the dog is coming in. Almost invariably a dog inclined to freeze will deliver quickly since he knows there's another job to do that will continue his contact with the handler. Do this repeatedly, making the throws shorter and shorter. The whole act will seem to have less importance and a final retrieve will usually be accomplished without freezing. If not,

This Springer shows the style and ideal technique in the delivery of a bird. Proper training is the key that makes this so. Photo by Evelyn Shafer.

just give a diverting wave of the hand without throwing the buck. This will do it, although it might be a breach of the rule against fooling a dog on a retrieve. This is an exception that is made to accomplish a definite purpose and you do not send the dog.

By no means should the handler play tug-of-war with a dog that freezes. Don't compete with the dog. Take the retrieve in one hand while commanding "give," and placing the other hand under the lower jaw, press the dogs lips between his teeth until he relinquishes his hold. With practice, this can become a one-handed operation with the lower hand, which can manage the bird as the dog drops it. The dog can thus be kept aware of the fact that the fingers may press his lips if the bird is not freely given up. Clever handlers can make the delivery of a recalcitrant dog look good.

8. Direction Signals

After a dog walks well at heel, hups when you stop or command or whistle a single blast, or on flush or shot, comes on recall and retrieves to hand, he should be taught to respond to direction signals. This will help you to guide him to a fall he may not have marked, and it will also aid in working out his hunting pattern.

There are several methods used successfully to get the idea across to a dog that he should move in the direction of your outstretched right or left arm and move further out when your arm is held overhead. Combinations of the methods may be used, of course. Most important is that you get response and not create confusion.

One method involves planting a retrieving buck a short distance to the right without the dog's knowledge. Now send the dog to fetch and walk a few steps to the right with your arm outstretched in that direction. The dog will start out but perhaps hesitate since he saw no fall. Command fetch again

Direction signals give the hunter better control over his dog in the field. They also make the dog more efficient in quartering and flushing birds.

A bold flushing dog should be able to hunt in any kind of cover. This Springer has just flushed the bird for the gun and is waiting to mark the fall.

This American Cocker has been guided to the pheasant's place of hiding by means of direction signals. He has now performed a bold flush and gotten the bird before the hunters' guns.

and walk a few more steps with your still outstretched arm. You may have to walk all the way to the retrieve before the dog finally realizes that there was a reason for the signal and picks it up. Run back to the starting point and accept the retrieve. Now, unbeknown to the dog, throw the buck out a bit further or at a slightly different angle. Repeat the arm swing with a few steps. You will find that the dog will catch on and move out in the direction of your action and make the retrieve with fewer attempts on your part. Repeat until the dog gets the idea. This is a good time to praise him and end the lesson.

During the next session repeat what has been learned once or twice and then do the same thing to the left. When both right and left hand lessons have been learned, try teaching straight away from you with an overhead signal.

Another method is to send a dog out on a thrown buck retrieve. As he comes in throw another buck to the right. Hup him upon receiving the buck, then send him to the right with a right hand signal. Repeat to right and left and back. Now, plant an unseen buck to the right. Throw it straight out or to the left and upon completion, order him to the right. Chances are he'll

This Springer is rearing up in the tall grass to let his handler know where he is and to get further signals.

These ladies are preparing to send their Cocker on to quarter a field for game. Hunting over a good direction taker makes for even greater enjoyment in the field.

Direction signals are as useful in water work as they are on land. Training a dog to take proper signals increases his value as a hunting companion no matter where he is worked.

move out that way and the buck will be there. Now, plant bucks left and right, then bring him to the line and throw one out. When he has delivered, order him to right and left for the planted bucks.

Next step is to plant bucks left or right or back or all three. Bring him to the line and send him without first sending him for a buck which he sees thrown.

When he takes directions this way, hup him, then walk a few feet back and send him from this relative position. Then work him from further and further away. When you have him taking the lines you give him you can command him in any direction.

Your next step is to start him and change his directions. To do this you must start him to the right, then hup him with a single blast and send him for the left retriever. Now you have a finished direction taker.

9. Introduction To Birds

DEVELOPING HUNTING ENTHUSIASM

It is quite possible that much of a dog's training can be done before actual introduction to game. This is fortunate, not only because seasons afield are often limited and many of us cannot afford the time and money that unlimited availability of game involves, but because a dog is not really ready physically to breast the natural cover of a game inhabited field and do so with sufficient power and stamina until he is at least five months old. Oftentimes six, seven or even eight months may be a better age for some individuals.

When a youngster is just taken into the field, with the hope, of course, that he will contact some kind of game, everything possible should be done to build up his enthusiasm. Let him hunt the likely places and hunt with him

Spaniels are, as a rule, naturally enthusiastic hunters. The introduction to birds should be done in such a way so the dog's zest for hunting is never dampened.

The American Water Spaniel is rare among field enthusiasts. This is unfortunate as the breed is possessed of great heart and makes an excellent retriever.

The finished, capable hunter is always a great thrill to the sportsman. Careful training in accustoming a dog to birds will add greatly to a dog's usefulness.

The dog that has been trained intelligently, using scents, good training dummies, feathers and shackled birds, will always be a dependable retriever.

The ruffed grouse is a favorite game of American hunters. Photo by Winchester-Western.

in the hope that one of you will flush game. It makes no difference what the game is. Rabbits or pheasant or lesser birds, anything that will get up and go and give the youngster a desire to hunt.

Let him chase anything he flushes. This is not the time to steady him or to discriminate between what is for the game bag and what isn't. It is only important that he finds out that by scouring the cover he can find exciting creatures that will increase the tempo of his tail. Chase with him if you like and do anything else that will increase his excitement. Later on, when there is no doubt about the way he gets out and goes in the field, you can start to use his yard breaking training to stop him on flush.

GAME TO USE FOR EXPERIENCE

Natural game is fine for training and to keep a trained dog in trim, but its availability is limited in numbers and in time. Professional trainers and amateur owners with means raise pheasants for the purpose or have holding pens in which to keep pheasants purchased for training. Such an operation usually requires a preserve permit of some sort.

Some shooting preserves make provision for training by providing grounds and birds by some arrangement. If one has available land, pheasants

An important part in teaching a young dog the basics of hunting is to take him out in the field and let him chase about after any game that is there. His zest for real hunting will be much heightened by this.

The woodcock is the game for which Cocker Spaniels were named. These birds are also much sought after by American sportsmen. Photo by Winchester-Western.

can be purchased from breeders for training. Gun clubs may have grounds suitable for training, on which purchased birds may be liberated.

Field trial officials usually sell the birds shot at the trial. A dead bird or two can be helpful. Retriever trials would likely have ducks as well as pheasants which could be purchased. A typical price for trial shot birds is one dollar and fifty cents for ducks, two dollars for pheasants and fifty cents for quail. Quail would more likely be available at a pointing dog trial where a bird or two could be had for the asking.

Ducks make the best game for water retrieving. A live duck, if properly shackled or sleeved with a knitted jacket to restrain wings and feet, can be used indefinitely if properly housed and fed, providing the dog has a soft mouth. Dog and duck often become great friends.

Pigeons are common substitutes for greater game. They are, of course, sporting marks in flight for the gun and if shackled will, like ducks, survive much training and become acclimated to the carrying of a soft mouthed dog. It is cheaper and easier to use live pigeons than other live birds. Homing pigeons, once a loft has become their home by virtue of mating, raising young or a few months stay, will return to the loft after being flushed. Thus they can be used repeatedly until, of course, they are shot. Homing pigeon racing fanciers often have birds available when they cull their stock. They

The correct introduction to birds will result in a dog who is enthusiastic to flush, mark, and retrieve.

Pigeons have proven useful to introduce young dogs to bird work. The owner of a loft will usually have a number of birds for sale, that can provide much training. Photo by Louise Van der Meid.

One can secure pheasants or partridges at a field trial. They can usually be had at low prices.

can sell certain birds they do not wish to keep because of repetition of bloodlines which can be bought for twenty-five or fifty cents.

If facilities permit, one can breed their own pigeons from a small start. Pigeons multiply rather rapidly and, between homing and breeding, a small loft can supply a lot of training.

PLANTING BIRDS FOR FLUSHING

It is common practice in field trials to plant pheasants (pigeons are often used in lesser stakes or fun trials) on the course so that there will be some kind of a guarantee of bird work every few minutes. Without this it might take hours to judge a single brace of dogs and field trials could not be as effective or popular as they are.

Bird planters, moving well ahead of the dogs, plant the birds in a manner that, by the guesswork of a good planter, will leave the bird to become fully conscious, recover its footing and be ready for a strong flush when it is located by the dog. Trainers can use the same methods, though they can modify the planting to their own timing, depending upon how long after planting their trainee should locate the bird.

Care must be used in handling birds for planting so that the bird is not injured or the planter scratched — particularly by feet. Pheasants, especially, being the strong runners that they are, have powerful legs and feet. Feet, wings and head must be held firmly. Everyone to his own best method, but one is to hold the bird's legs with the right hand and hold the wings closed with the left, running the hand down until wings and legs can be encompassed by the right hand. Now, extending the neck gently to its full length, tuck the head under one wing without twisting. Stroke the birds breast with the left hand and set the bird down gently, with feet extended backward, and walk away quietly. It will take the bird several seconds to regain consciousness and it will then proceed to orient itself and get its feet under it in preparation for flying or running. By this time the dog should be approaching and the impending location and flush should follow.

If more time is needed, use the same technique but plant the bird on its back or swing it gently in a circle ten or a dozen times before planting. Pigeons can be similarly planted with less risk of their running off.

The Canada goose is an all-time favorite for waterfowl hunters. A strong dog with great determination can usually bring one of these birds in.

Perhaps the most popular upland game bird in the United States is the ringneck pheasant. The sly ringneck is a worthy opponent in the field and a worthy addition to the hunter's table. Photo by Wisconson Conservation Department.

PRACTICE TRAILING CRIPPLES

Many times in the hunting life of a dog he will be faced with the task of locating birds which he has marked down (seen fall) but which were not killed and retained the use of both legs. A good nose and prompt action will enable the dog to run such cripples down and retrieve them to hand. This is one of the very valuable assets of a flushing spaniel. The wings of a bird can be bound carefully and the bird released to run. Put the dog on the line (line of the birds escape route) and command him to fetch. Such practice in trailing is invaluable.

Do not do this with dogs that are not already experienced in retrieving birds as a youngster might lose a lot of his enthusiasm for the work if he is spurred by a pheasant. There might also be the risk of his becoming hard mouthed or a blinker.

10. Final Essentials

Since the flushing dog must work within gun range to be of use to the hunter, it is important that he develop a more or less regular pattern of swings to right and left as he quarters the ground. Differences in cover and wind will, of course, make deviations from the regularity of the pattern logical for the most effective searching for game. Generally speaking, the dog should run in a series of arcs with a radius of fifteen to twenty-five yards, moving forward as he changes direction so as to make the next arc about as far forward of the last as the handler walks in the time involved.

If we assume that the dog has been taken afield and been in contact with game, either wild or planted, so he knows there is something to seek, we need only modify the pattern of his seeking.

The field trial has become an important part of the American sporting scene. Dogs like Roy French's Kansan have distinguished themselves by turning in polished performances, which were the result of careful training.

Smooth technique never ceases to please. This dog is accomplishing a faultless delivery. The trainer can be proud of this student.

A well-schooled dog will seek birds on his own initiative, and under the direction of those he is hunting with.

The dog has been taught to respond to direction signals, so we cast him off with a swing of the arm and a few steps in the direction we intend for the first cast. When he has run far enough out, blow the whistle. (One short blast is now being used to stop the dog. Traditionally two short toots are used to turn a dog while quartering.) The dog will stop and look at you. Sweep an arm and take a few steps in the other direction. After a few times the dog will probably make change of direction without any more than hesitating while you signal. With still more practice, he will continue to run as he changes direction. Finally, he will make the change of direction automatically without change of pace when he hears the two whistle blasts. An experienced dog will, thereafter, learn to adjust the length of his casts and need help from the whistle but occasionally.

Be careful not to get the dog into too restricted a range. Out of range, of course, is bad, but working underfoot without reasonable reach for objectives so restricts a dog's pattern as to greatly reduce the amount of territory he can cover for you in a given time.

If you can find a field that is fenced at about the ideal width of a good pattern, it will aid materially in getting a dog to swing as he should.

There is a special enjoyment in hunting when the air carries the crisp snap of winter, and the senses of dogs and men are sharpened by the invigorating cold. Photo by Evelyn Shafer.

Though the practice is not common, some hunters use a brace of dogs in the field. Photo by Louise Van der Meid.

Remember, once a dog is working well for you, limit the number of commands or whistles you use to a minimum. A dog has much more initiative if not overhandled and the pleasure of working a dog that doesn't have to be turned at the end of every cast is much greater.

Whenever cover is irregular or the direction of travel such that a piece of cover is being neglected, a responsive dog can be sent to or through it with ease. Sometimes the wind may be blowing from the gun to a stone wall or hedgerow, in which event the dog should be on the far side of it to work it to best advantage and to increase the chances of flushing the bird toward the gun.

INTRODUCTION TO THE GUN

Many recommendations have been written advising that introduction to gunfire should start with firing twenty-two blanks when the dog is feeding and gradually decreasing the distance and then increasing the bore and size of the load until the dog becomes accustomed to, shall we say, a typical 12 gauge pheasant load. It is my feeling that the most important thing is that the dog be at a reasonable distance and enthusiastically flushing a bird when the gun is fired. It is a rare dog that will be disturbed by a twenty gauge at twenty yards when he has just pushed the bird into the air and still has his eyes full of tail feathers, snoot full of scent and ears full of wing beat.

The Cocker Spaniel, the "ideal gentleman's shooting dog," has been providing sport and pleasure to hunters for several centuries. More people discover the sport of hunting every year.

Ruth Greening, Mrs. Albert Winslow, and Gene Hutchins (from l. to r.) members of the Ladies Amateur Spaniel Handlers' Association, with three American Cockers, one English Cocker, and three English Springers. All of the breeds pictured are capable field dogs and each is a great favorite of American hunters.

Many trainers use a twenty-two blank to condition their pupils to gun fire. They also help to associate the gun fire to a fall so the dog will immediately anticipate the excitement of a retrieve when he hears a shot. This can be worked in well with retrieving practice.

Start by throwing a buck in the usual retrieving practice manner. Now, have a helper throw the buck as you handle the dog. When the dog is accustomed to this, have the handler move out so he is facing you and the dog at a distance of about twenty yards. After he has thrown one or two bucks and the dog has made single and double retrieves from this system, have the assistant fire a blank and then throw. Each time thereafter he will fire the blank and then throw the buck. This is excellent retrieving practice.

Now, with the handler at a distance, out front or to the side: Choose a time when the dog is looking elsewhere, then the gun is fired and the buck thrown. The gun will swing the dog's attention to the fall of the buck so he will be able to mark it. If you wish you may have two assistants — one to left and one to right, whichever throws a buck to be marked fires the blank first and then throws. The dog will soon learn that a shot means a fall and will look in order to mark it. He will come to anticipate the shot with pleasure, since he will have learned that the shot is associated with his work, which a good dog enjoys.

When a dog has been working enthusiastically on either a training buck or birds, the magnitude of the shot can be increased until it is that of the loads usually used in hunting. It is a grave error to overdo. Never shoot too close to a dog or with loads or guns (unusually short-barrelled smoothbores, for example) that make unusually loud reports. Even if it doesn't make a dog gunshy, it can be very painful to his ears.

SPORT OF HUNTING WITH A FLUSHING DOG

Now that your dog has been trained to travel with you in civilized fashion, to enter the hunting or trial field with you at your side, to quarter the ground enthusiastically and systematically when cast off, to hup at flush or shot, mark the fall and retrieve to hand over land or water on command, you, too, have learned some very important things. One of these is the very sporting difference between gunning over a flushing dog in comparison to a pointer.

The pointing dog hunter, though his mind and heart are with his dog as he directs the hunt, and the thrill of a dog suddenly freezing on point is a thing never to be forgotten, need not be on his toes every moment as does his flushing dog counterpart. He has time to get to his dog, flush the bird at

The well-trained flushing spaniel can be a dual provider, bringing trophies for the den and meat for the table.

The owner of the well trained field dog may truly be proud. His dog is the practitioner of a skill that is almost as old as the needs of man itself.

leisure, being ready, meanwhile, for the shot. The flushing dog hunter must be forever on the alert for the rise of a bird. His dog must be kept within gun range at all times. Changes in pace must be matched when runners are encountered that cause a dog to line out in pursuit, which, if not quick may be fruitless. That ever-busy spaniel tail must be under constant observation. By watching one end of the dog the gun knows what's going on at the other. Suddenly, what the nose knows the eyes confirm and the dog rushes in to push the bird into flight. The gun must be alert in order that the dog may make the job complete to bring back trophies for the den or meat for the table.

Recommended Reading

Breed Your Dog, Dr. Leon Whitney, 64 pp., $1.00. Illustrated throughout with instructive photographs in both color and black and white. Covers aspects of breeding through puppyhood.
Dollars In Dogs, Leon F. Whitney, D.V.M., 255 pp., $4.95. Twenty-six chapters on different vocations in the vast field of dog business. An excellent book for your library.
First Aid For Your Dog, Dr. Herbert Richards, 64 pp., $1.00. Illustrated throughout in both color and black and white.
Groom Your Dog, Leon F. Whitney, D.V.M., 64 pp., $1.00. Illustrated throughout with both color and black and white photographs showing various grooming techniques.
How To Feed Your Dog, Dr. Leon F. Whitney, 64 pp., $1.00. Best diets and feeding routines for puppies and adult canines. Profusely illustrated in color and black and white.
How To Housebreak And Train Your Dog, Arthur Liebers, 80 pp., $1.00. Six educational chapters on training your dog. Illustrated in color and black and white photographs.
How To Raise And Train A Pedigreed Or Mixed Breed Puppy, Arthur Liebers, 64 pp., $1.00. Nine chapters covering such canine questions as choosing your puppy through breeding the adult. Illustrated in both color and black and white photographs.
How To Show Your Dog, Virginia Tuck Nichols, 252 pp., $4.95. This book is written for the novice who plans to show his dog. An excellent text to make your dog library complete.
The Distemper Complex, Leon F. Whitney, D.V.M., and George D. Whitney, D.V.M., 219 pp., $5.00. A comprehensive canine health book. Nineteen revealing chapters. A thirty-nine-page bibliography. Completely indexed.
This Is The Puppy, Ernest Hart, 190 pp., $4.95. Eleven profusely-illustrated chapters to guide the reader in the care and selection of a puppy. Full-color photographs. Also black and white candids. Indexed.